Privies *of* Wales

Other books by J.Aelwyn Roberts

In English:

The Privies of North Wales
The Holy Ghostbuster
Yesterday's People

In Welsh:

Andalusia
Yr Anhyaoel
Pobol Ddoe

In Portuguese:

Viver Com Fantasmas

Privies *of* Wales

J. Aelwyn Roberts

Tegai Publications

Published in Wales by
Tegai Publications,
Haulfre Vicarage,
Llandegai
Bangor LL57 4LA
Tel: 01248 353711

ISBN 0-9539494-0-0

Printed and bound in Wales by:
MWL Print Group
Pontypool
Telephone: 01495 750033

CONTENTS

Thank You

It is my name on the cover; but I have acted more as editor than I have as author. It is the dozens of people from all over Wales who have written to me about their privies, and about their "tales of the good old days", who are the real authors. I raise my hat in gratitude to them all.

I thank CADW for its generous grant towards the publishing of the book. My first book on the," Privies of North Wales", is still selling so well that it is doubtful whether a second book, on the same subject, would have attracted a publisher without a guarantee of a subsidy.

Grant apart Janette Watson, of CADW, has been so supportive and helpful through out the period of researching and writing. Rosemary Jones of the Royal Commission on the Ancient and Historical Monuments of Wales has also given a great deal of help.

I have to thank the Happy Guild of Privy Owners for their 'CROESO' and also for the knowledge and information supplied by organisations like :-

The National Library of Wales

St Fagan's Museum of Welsh Life

The Roman Legion Museum in Caerleon

The Victoria and Albert Museum

The Ironbridge Gorge Museum

The staff of the National Trust both North and South Wales

Many of the these staff officials like Margaret Evans of The South Wales National Trust, and her colleague Nicky Evans of the Llannerch Aeron Trust, have become friends and cheerful helpers. Many others like Susan Balance, who lives at beautiful Abercamlais, has walked with me much further than the biblical mile.

I must say a special "Thank You" to the Western Mail. Books such as this one cannot be sold, or researched, without the help of a good newspaper. The Western Mail told its South Wales readers what I was about and the readers responded.

My old friend Chloris Morgan, in school-mam fashion, has again presided over all my syntax failings.

But this time it is my son Mark who deserves the Medal of Honour. Whilst I was thumping away at the text on my computer in the one room, he was in the next designing the book cover and four of the most delightful coloured illustrations. I kept going from one room to the to next just to have another little peep at his work. I know my readers will enjoy them.

I only hope that all of you who have so willingly contributed towards the making of this book will be happy with the way I have tried to put it together.

J. Aelwyn Roberts

I

I am the Prologue

꒞

TWO years ago Nicholas Battle, publisher of Countryside Books, invited me to write a book on *"The Privies of North Wales"*. My immediate reaction was one of No! No! No! This was not my scene.

But Nicholas Battle is a good and persuasive diplomat. He went on to tell me that he was virtually giving me the opportunity to write a book that would be read by generations to come. He was inviting me to write a *classic*. He suggested I could be to *Welsh Privies* what George Borrow is to *Wales*. He elaborated that if I wrote a book on the privies of North Wales for his publishing firm no other publishing firm in the country would touch the subject for at least another twenty years. And in twenty years, he said, "there will be no privies in North Wales for anyone to write about". I am a vain person. I have always wanted to be the author of a *classic*. The book was written and was very well received.

Nicholas Battle was right in his assessment of the future of these old privies. He himself had made up his mind, years ago, to do something about it. He has used his publishing firm to engage authors to write about the privies of their own areas. He has already published more than a dozen books covering the greater part of England. They are the *Cotswold Privies, East Anglian Privies, Kent Privies, Hampshire Privies* and many, many more. There were times when commissioned writers wrote back to him to say: "Sorry but there are no old privies in my area for me to write about. They've all been demolished".

Apart from my book, *"The Privies of North Wales"*, there was not even a leaflet available anywhere in Wales about the romance and the smells, the tranquillity and intimacy that emanated from these old institutions. Many elderly people, to this day, describe privies as belonging to the "good old days". But no one has yet managed to say why.

Whilst researching the first book, an official of the National Trust said to me: "It was whilst searching for information for your book that I realised how very few of the many old houses we administer have retained their garden toilets."

Friends from south and mid-Wales reminded me that they, too, had a number of the endangered privies in their part of the world and that they, too, cared for the things of "by-gone days" but they had no way of keeping them in remembrance.

In desperation I wrote to CADW—a Welsh heritage trust—to warn them of the great catastrophe that was befalling us. I soon found that I was preaching to the converted. Within five days of my sending the letter CADW offered me a generous research grant to bring out a sort of 'Book of Remembrance ' about privies and to commemorate the debt we owe to these old closets. I rolled up my sleeves and began to work. I was amazed at the response.

The bad news is that more and more of our old privies are being demolished year by year.

The good news is that more and more people who have become owners of houses where garden privies are a feature are so proud of their new acquisitions that they are spending time and money renovating them. Estate agents are also getting round to the idea that a property with a 19th Century privy, in a good state of repair, is an asset worth mentioning in the advertising blurb when a house is being sold.

I find that privy owners are a breed apart. They are so proud of their privies. They love it when you ask if you can come and see them. When you take your camera out of its case they seem to edge closer to the loo so that they too can appear in the shot. But the strangest thing about owning a garden privy is that friends and neighbours seem to bask in the reflected glory of the ownership. Whenever I have advertised for knowledge of old privies most of the replies received in return have been: "Dear Sir. Our friends/neighbours have a lovely privy which I think you should see". These are letters full of vicarious pride and a little envy.

So, in the words of the famous stockbrokers Hargreaves, Hargreaves and Hargreaves I would say:

"If you have shares in earth, bucket, or any other old privy, our advice is HOLD. The bear market in old, bottom of the garden, privies may be levelling out ".

As a retired clergyman I know only too well the difficulty Hon. Secs. of various clubs and associations have finding speakers for their monthly meetings. If anyone formed an *Antique Privy Owner's Society* there would be no problem. Members of this Society could keep themselves going for months just swapping their own quaint lavatory tales. This is one I am itching to tell.

Richard Ellis-Davies is a very old friend of mine. He celebrated his ninetieth birthday some years ago. Richard was a family solicitor and, for many years, was Deputy High Sheriff of Caernarfonshire. But this story concerns his childhood. His father was Member of Parliament for Caernarfon Boroughs during the period of the First World War when Lloyd George represented Caernarfonshire in the Commons. Ellis-Davies senior would come home from Westminster by train every Friday night and return on Monday morning. He would always bring with him, from his London office, an abundance of scrap paper for the children to draw on or to be cut up and used in the privy.

One Friday evening the MP dad brought home with him two high ranking fellow Members of Parliament, together with the usual pack of waste paper. His wife, taken aback by the arrival of two unexpected guests, handed the bundle of papers to Rosie the maid saying: "We can manage without that lot for a start. Take all this paper down to the Ty Bach, Rosie. Don't bother to cut it into squares; we can do that next week. Just take it out of the way for now".

Rosie toddled off with the paper and was back in no time. An hour or so later, one of the London VIP's wended his way to the garden and towards the Little House at the bottom. He sauntered slowly as was the custom, bent down to smell each little rose, and ran his hand through the tufts of lavender and rosemary growing in profusion along the path. In two minutes he was back, doubled-up with laughter.

When the others in the drawing room saw him, they went to ask the cause of such merriment. But the big man could only point towards the loo and continue his howls of laughter. So the whole party toddled along into the spacious privy; and there it was on the wall as they entered.

Patriotic Rosie, taking the papers, had noted that some of them were war recruiting posters and thought it would be such a shame to use such posters as bottom-wipes. So she had carefully pasted one of them on to the wall. It was a picture of a rather ancient General Roberts displaying the Victoria Cross he had won in the Boer War. Under the picture, the words proclaimed:

HE DID HIS DUTY.   WILL YOU DO YOURS!

I have only one more thing to say before we enter into the complexities of man's lavatorial behaviour through five million years existence on planet earth. It is about the name of the place we are about to study … *The Privy*. Having been born and brought up in Blaenau Ffestiniog, the word 'privy' is alien to me. In the Blaenau of my day—where Welsh was not just our first but our only language—we used to refer to the place as "*Y Ty Bach*", or "The Little House. Although I left Blaenau nearly 60 years ago, it is quite amazing that when I type the word 'Privy', I still catch myself mouthing its Welsh equivalent, "*Ty Bach*".

I have been amazed also that so many of my fellow English writers on the subject of Privies are able to produce very nearly a hundred names for the same place. We in Wales are far more conservative and more limited in our terminology. And if I may say so, we are also a little more delicate in our way of describing things pertaining to the posterior parts of our bodies than are our friends across Offa's Dyke. We refuse to use the equivalent of what we would regard as rather crude Anglo Saxon terminology. I can think of only a few privy names that are in common usage in Wales:

"Ty Bach" The "Little House" is by far the most common name.

"Lle Chwech" the "Sixpenny Place", that still baffles me. I remember some years ago being invited as an 'expert' by the BBC to give a talk on "Old Privies". Hywel Gwynfryn was the interviewer. His first question was: "Tell me Aelwyn why do we in Wales call these old privies "Y Lle Chwech?" The BBC's *expert* was stumped. With hindsight I realise this was possibly the first time in my long history of broadcasting that I had failed to waffle my way out of a difficult question. I had to say that I hadn't got a clue. I still don't.

"Ty Cyffredin", "Houses of Parliament" was also a popular name. "Number 10", presumably Downing Street, was another.

"Mynd i'r cefn", "Going to the back quarters" was also a favourite way of putting it.

There was also the more regal way of excusing yourself; "I'm just going to make a call to *Buckingham Palace*"!

II

The Long Dark Age

5,000,000 BC to 1850 AD

Piltdown Man

If anyone was asked to write the Sanitary History of mankind from the earliest times to the end of the second millennium it would appear to be a formidable task. But it shouldn't be. For during the first five million years of Sanitary History, absolutely nothing at all happened for anyone to write about. If we accept that the first man came to live on earth about five million years ago the sanitary historian would just write: *"And when the first Adams, and the first Eves, felt the need to relieve themselves, they would just walk a short distance away from their dwelling place, dig a hole, defecate into it, wipe their bottoms with tufts of grass or moss, cover the hole with soil, and walk away"*.

And that was how things remained for more than five million years. Dig hole, do your business, cover the hole, and walk away. If one wished to be meticulous one could say that there was possibly just a slight bit of progress, at some time during this long period. The very earliest dwellers on earth, we are told, and I have no idea by whom, dug up the ground around their homes, but in the summer, when the air became pungent, they would move their dwellings a few yards further away from last year's dung heaps. After three million years they decided to make their homes permanent and their privies movable.

14

Throughout this barren reporting period for the sanitary historian, his contemporary, the social historian, has so much to say and explain. Was there a time when man did not stand erect? At what stage did he begin to stand erect? When did he first learn how to use fire? How did he come to invent the wheel? When did he discover metal? Who was the first person in Europe to be able to melt it and make tools of it? What language did he use?

There follows for the social historian that exciting period of great mysteries and great challenges right through the Renaissance, with its beautiful paintings, and literature, and works of art; and the Industrial Revolution with its great discoveries, and inventions, like those of James Hargreaves' Spinning Jenny, that changed lives, and fortunes almost overnight. But even as the social historian is describing the excitement of the birth of steam and the work of the pioneers, James Watt and George Stevenson, opening the first railway in the world, to run from Stockton to Darlington, the only comment the poor old sanitary historian would be able to make would be; *"and when these great inventors, James Watt and George Stevenson, felt the need to relieve themselves they and their workpeople would go, singly, to a place apart, dig a hole etc"*.

The poor sanitary historian, for his part, would have nothing new to report until the beginning of the nineteenth century, when newspapers started to appear in libraries and in homes. He would then report that, as from about 1800, when newspapers began to appear, the richer people were beginning to change the materials they had used to wipe their bottoms for the last five million years. He would report that they no longer used odd bits of material, tufts of grass or moss, or soft river stones, but that they now used, the newly invented newsprint cut into small squares.

It is true that by the 16th and the 17th Centuries some of the county families had ventured to introduce indoor closets into their dwellings. With their large, airy, houses they could afford to. However in spite of its name, the *'Inside Closet'*, it was in fact nothing more than what we today would call a bucket commode. They had the servants carry away the contents at regular intervals. In 1745, Dean Jonathan Swift, published a most courageous essay, entitled "Directions to Servants". He berates the mistress who refuses to use the outside privy.

"I am much offended with those ladies, who are so proud, and lazy, that they will not be at pains to go into the garden and pick a rose (i.e. go into the garden privy), but keep an odious implement, sometimes in the bed chamber itself, or at least in a dark closet adjoining, which they make use of to ease their worse necessities, and you are the usual carriers away of the pan, which makes not only the chamber but their clothes offensive to all who come near. Now to cure them of the odious practice, let me advise you, on whom this offis lieth to convey away this utensil, that you do it openly down the great stairs, in the presence of the footmen: and if any knocketh, you open the street door whilst you still have the vessel in your hands: this if anything can and will make your lady take the pains of evacuating her person in the proper place (i.e outside the house), rather than expose her filthiness to all the men servants in the house".

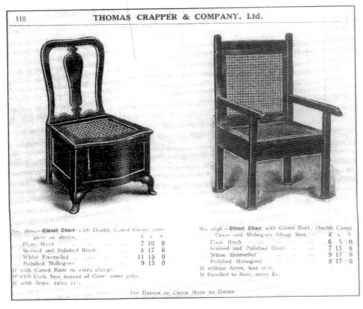

110 THOMAS CRAPPER & COMPANY, Ltd.

		£	s.	d.
No. 1610.—Closet Chair with Double Caned Cover, complete as shown.				
Plain Birch		7	10	0
Stained and Polished Birch		8	17	6
White Enamelled		11	15	0
Polished Mahogany		9	15	0
If with Caned Back no extra charge.				
If with Cork Seat instead of Cane, same price.				
If with Arms, extra 21/-.				

		£	s.	d.
No. 1658.—Closet Chair with Caned Back, Double Caned Cover and Mahogany liftup Seat.				
Plain Birch		6	5	0
Stained and Polished Birch		7	15	6
White Enamelled		9	17	6
Polished Mahogany		8	17	6
If without Arms, less 10/6.				
If Panelled to floor, extra £1.				

ANY DESIGN OF CHAIR MADE TO ORDER.

16

But the great majority of the people continued to dig holes, fill them, and walk away.

We know, and we honour, the names of men and women of the 19th Century who designed fine furniture, and painted lovely pictures, but we have no idea of the identity of the man, or woman, who invented the EARTH CLOSET. This great invention was one that came, like all other great inventions, when the need was greatest. The population of Britain in Tudor times was thought to be between four and five million people. By the middle of the 17th Century this had grown significantly. The land could no longer afford the luxury of a separate hole for each visit to the loo. Even people, with their own gardens, living in the country, were beginning to feel the pinch. The earth closet became popular around the 1850s. There had, however, been isolated examples of earth closets from very early days. We know for instance, that Newgate Jail in Blackfriars, London, had a very large earth privy as early as the 13th Century. It was only emptied when the stench became unbearable to the inmates and all that lived for miles around.

There is an extant record of a clean-out at Newgate in the year 1281. It took 13 men five nights to carry out the work. They were paid what was at that time, the princely sum of four pounds, seven shillings and eight pence. We also know of a gongfermor called Richard the Raker who designed an earth closet for his own use. In the year 1326 the poor man met with a dreadful death. He fell through the rotten planks of his privy seat and "drowned, monstrously, in his own excrement".

The basic idea of an earth closet was simple. Instead of home dwellers digging numberless little holes in their garden, they were now encouraged to dig one deep hole or trench. Planks were laid across this deep hole. Relief was obtained by sitting or crouching on the planks. Earth Closet, Mark II, had posterior sized holes cut into the planks and in a still later edition the planks were raised on platforms so that they resembled seats—seats with holes. After each usage the user was required to cover his excrement, down in the hole below, with soil. It was reckoned that a well dug, well maintained, earth closet would last a year before it needed emptying and when full would contain two and a half tons of soil and excrement. But when the day of the emptying did arrive it cast its doom over the whole family. The trench would become fuller and fuller, smellier and smellier, as the head of the household put off the evil day. It was a task too strenuous for most people. More often than not it required the service of a raker or a gongfermor (a word derived from the Saxon 'gong' meaning a private place, and 'fey', meaning to cleanse). In Welsh the closet service man was called the 'pannwr' or the 'carthiwr'. This help was costly, as these special workers demanded very high payment. The flat rate for emptying the new earth privies of the 1860s was £2. This was far beyond the means of manual workers and widows. So there were many who could not afford the high cost of maintaining the modern earth toilets. Earth toilets had been experimented with in the towns long before they became commonplace. There is a report of an accident to a Jewish gentleman, as early as 1516, which resembles, and calls to mind, our strict Welsh Sabbath rules of yesteryear:

"In this year also fell that happe of the Jew of Tewkesbury which fell into a gong upon the Saturday, and would not for reverence of the Sabot day be pulled out, whereof hearing, the Earle of Gloucester, that the Jew did so grete reverence to his sabot day, thought he would do as much to his holyday, which was Sunday, and so kept him there till Monday at which season he was foundyn dead." Poor soul.

The earth privy of the mid 19th Century must have been a wonderful innovation, and had been welcomed by rich and poor alike in spite of the fact that it was always smelly and, in the summer months, fly infested. Even royalty had to put up with smelly cesspits. Mary Queen of Scots wrote a letter from her prison in Tutbury Castle, Staffordshire:-

"As no house, with so many low bred people in it as this can be kept clean, however orderly they may be, so this house, and I blush to say it, wanting proper conveniences for the necessities of nature, has a sickening stench ever lingering in it. On every Saturday, too, the cess-

pools must be cleared out, even to the one below my windows, whence come non of the perfumes of Arabia."

It appears also that King Henry III was rather fastidious in matters of personal hygiene. Before he visited the homes of any of his barons he would have his Chamberlain write a letter to them about the kind of sanitary arrangements the King would expect of his hosts. A copy of these instructions can be found in John Russell's Book of Nature written in the 15th Century.

"See that the privy house for easement be fayre soot and cleane. And the bordes this be upon be covered with cloth fair and green. And the whole himself look there be no board be seen, Thereon a fair cushion the ardure no man to teme. Look there be blankit cotyn or linen to wipe the nether end."

These deep dug earth privies reigned supreme for half a century. In the mid-1900s another brilliant new idea emerged. This was the bucket privy. Many of the old earth trenches were concreted over. A bucket was then placed over the newly concreted floor. The earth privy seat, with one or more holes in it, was adapted to sit over the bucket space.

Buildings were erected around them and they became proper *"ty bachs"*. They weren't as cold or draughty or as smelly as the earth type. There was less irritation from flies; and the rat problem was reduced because the buckets had fitted lids to place over them when not in use. The mid-19th Century's *"ty bach"* became a cosy little place apart. It even had a little niche to hold a candle, or small lantern, for evening visitors.

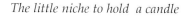

The little niche to hold a candle

And there was no further need to pay high emptying fees to the gongfermor. It seems amazing to think that with the coming of the covered bucket lavatory, the people of Wales, and all the people of Europe, believed that they had reached the utopia of lavatorial comfort. They asked for nothing more. In fact they fought hard, for the next half century, to prevent any further intrusion into their new life of luxury.

An old contemporary told me that he remembered his father building a family Ty Bach and adding to it a "Gentlemen Only" annex. The annex consisted of two corrugated iron sheets at the side. This was meant as a male urinal. Users were to aim at a hole in the middle that drained their wee into the field below. There always had been an unwritten law, both with earth and bucket closets, that it was not quite cricket for men and boys to use them just to wee in. Males would walk to the bottom of the garden, look around, and if at all possible urinate against a tree or a bush. It was the liquid content that took up most room in both the earth trench and the bucket. But Mrs Elin Williams of Newport, Gwent, tells me that when she was a child—the youngest of three girls—even they as girls were warned to use the privy only for "Number Two". If they just wanted to wee then they were to do it in the garden. They obviously had an earth privy at a time when everyone else was changing , or had changed, to a bucket privy because she goes on to tell me how her older sisters used to frighten her by saying that if she walked behind the Ty Bach she would sink in the domen (bog) right up to her neck.

The bucket system saw Britain through two world wars and remained in many places, until the second half of the twentieth century. The difference was that those who held on to their buckets until the 1960s, were not required to empty their own. Bucket emptying had, by now, become a service offered free to all householders by local authorities. The Council raker made his weekly collection visits in Amlwch Port, Anglesey, until as late as the 1960s.

But to the two main toilet systems of Britain, one has to add a third. These were the over-the-stream toilets. If I can paraphrase the Bible:

"Wise is the man who buildeth his House of Easement over water for he shall need neither earth nor bucket to dispose of his excrement". There is no doubt that a great number of dwelling sites were specially chosen near streams with the streams acting as sewers. Monastaries, particularly, were always built near fast flowing streams. There were probably more over-the-stream toilets in Wales than in any other part of Britain, except possibly Scotland, because Wales has such an abundance of mountain streams and rivers.

Over stream privy at Penmachno Mill doubles as Bidet when river is in flood

The teaching of history can be quite a complicated business. When our English neighbours speak of the 5th and the 6th Centuries they describe them as the beginning of the Dark Ages. Teachers in Welsh classrooms, however, describe the same period, to their pupils, as "The Golden Age of Saints". In exactly the same way when the sanitary historian describes all those years up to the 1900s as the Dark Ages in sanitary history, people living in the Austrian Alps, and the French Pyrenees, and in the Snowdonia National Park, and in the Brecon Beacons, would ask, "What Dark Ages?"

A happy water privy

These are the people who lived where multitudinous streams ran down from the mountains. All they had to do to relieve themselves was walk on to the sturdy oak planks across the stream that ran through their garden. They knew of no smells and were not burdened by rakings. When, eventually, Ty Bachs were built over their stream planks, they asked no more. They were a contented people.

There are today, at the beginning of a new millennium, still thousands of people—and I count myself amongst them—who are not connected to any Local Authority main sewerage system. Main sewerage even in the year 2000 has not yet arrived at our village. But we have our own, private, septic tanks. This is something one can describe as a remodelled, rejuvenated, renovated model of the old earth toilet. The toilet and plumbing in the house is like any other modern toilet but the effluence is piped into a tank buried in the garden. These tanks don't smell and the need to empty them should only arise every 30 or 40 years. They function on the same principle as deep litter in the hen-house or a piggery. The bacteria in the tank somehow kills and devours its own smells and effluence. These septic tanks are most efficient. If the Water Board ever does catch up with those of us who live in remote areas and invites us to connect up to their new sewerage scheme, it is possible that many of us will be as reluctant to accept their invitation as our parents were to forfeit their Tai Bachs. With our own septic tanks, we enjoy the same *mod cons* as our neighbours, but without having to pay the monstrous sewage charges levied by the Water Board.

Modern septic tanks are recognised, today, as being environmentally safe and friendly. 150 years ago they were anything but safe or friendly. During the 19th Century the Cathedral City of Bangor, in Gwynedd, had a very poor medical record. Its populace, greatly expanded with the coming of the railway and the expansion of the slate quarries, suffered recurring, debilitating, illnesses, and many died. There were those who contended that the cause of the illness was contaminated drinking water. In 1854 the City Fathers, at great cost, began the construction of a new water system for Bangor. Clean water was piped to Bangor, from Afon Caseg in the mountains above Bethesda. The water was stored in a covered reservoir on Bangor Mountain and from there dispensed its blessings to the houses below. But far from abating the illnesses of Bangor the new water works seemed to aggravate them. So much so that they became known as the Bangor Plagues, "Clwy Bangor". The costly water works had done nothing except, perhaps, wrongly persuade people that their plagues were airborne, and not water borne. They could not possibly be the result of polluted water, now that the expensive new water system had been installed. In the 1870s John Williams, head clerk at the Penrhyn Estate, who was father to seven children, extended his kitchen at his home in Penlan, Llandegai, because he believed that the illness thrived in cramped crowded conditions.

1882 was the year when aldermen and councillors throughout North Wales were canvassing the suitability of their town to become the seat of the new University College of North Wales. Geographically the Cathedral City of Bangor seemed the most likely choice. But its opponents argued that Bangor was a sick city, unfit for young people to live in.

In the May of this crucial year, Bangor was stuck by another of its plagues more terrible and more violet than any of its predecessors. Over 700 of its inhabitants were struck with fever and suffered for many weeks; 48 people died. A month after the outbreak a young Dr Rees, newly appointed M.O.H. for Bangor,

The University College of North Wales

claimed that he had discovered the source of Bangor's troubles. He maintained that the cause of the plague was a seepage of human and animal sewage from a farm called Llwynrhandir that had been allowed to contaminate the Bangor water. As a matter of fact the first casualty of this latest infection was a member of the Llwynrhandir family. The farm was situated a few yards above the spot where Dr Rees had reported that both animal and human sewage from the farm filtered into the river and into the Bangor drinking water. He suggested a simple remedy, that a trench be dug to carry the farm's sewage away from the river. But this was anathema to the City Fathers. They had spent so much money on their new Water Works. They rejected their officer's report and called in an expert. The expert completed his report in the August, and agreed absolutely with young Dr Rees' diagnosis, and with his treatment suggestions. The trench was dug; the plague was extinguished. There is no doubt that if the proud city aldermen had accepted, and acted on, the recommendation of the young Dr Rees many of the 48, who died, would have been saved. But his report, corroborated by the expert, did arrive in time for Bangor to be able to persuade the university senate that Bangor's sickness problems were at an end. Two years later, in 1884, building began on the University College of North Wales on a hill overlooking the Cathedral.

This is just one of many stories that tell how people throughout Wales suffered and died, of typhoid, and cholera, and other water-borne illnesses. Children in particular. This particular example, of the damage that gallons of clean mountain water, mixed with a suspicion of sewage, can do to human health in a rural area, makes one cringe at the thought of how much greater the damage was in the cities, where water was mixed with hundreds of gallons of human sewage. London, and other cities, were forever plague ridden. The richer people escaped the infection by moving to the country; the poorer people stayed, and died by the hundreds, and were buried in mass graves.

Town dwellers, from the beginning of time, not fortunate enough to be living near a running stream, or to possess the tiniest of gardens, were compelled to resort to 'Plan Four'. They bought buckets, or slop pails, or chamber pots—lots of them. These were all kept inside the house. Buckets, and the slop pails, and the chamber pots, used in overcrowded dwellings, were soon filled to the brim. Several times a day the householder would simply open the bedroom window or the front door and very much as the modern golfer gives one shout of his intent, the 18th Century householder would give one shout of "Gardy-loo"—*Gardez-l'eau*—(Watch for Water) and throw the utensil's contents, on to the pavement, or on to the pedestrian below, for the wind and the rain to dispel. The poet Dryden in 1650 wrote of the dangers of perambulating the streets of the town at night:-

> *"Tis want of sense to sup abroad too late*
> *Unless thou first hast settled thine estate.*
> *As many fates attend thy steps to meet*
> *As there are waking windows in the streets.*
> *Bless the good gods and think thy chance is rare*
> *To have a piss pot only, for thy share."*

It might be true to say that the period after the Industrial Revolution in the 18th Century, that had seen the great population movement from country to town, also saw the time when Britain had more slop bucket *garde* loos, than it had earth or bucket privies. It is difficult for us to imagine the awful smells that both rich, and poor, had to endure whilst walking the street of towns and cities. Ladies in posh crinoline dresses and gentlemen in their coloured waistcoats and silk hats constantly ran the risk of having the contents of a chamber pot thrown over them as they walked the pavements below. And yet, and this is the part that is so difficult to understand, both rich and poor categorically and unequivocally rejected the very idea of having a toilet inside the house where they lived and where they ate their meals. It never ceases to amaze me that even recently, up to about 50 years ago, members of different families in this country would have sat, enthralled, in front of their television sets, watching the first man landing on the moon, and then afterwards, would have strolled quite nonchalantly to the bottom of the garden to do *poo* in a bucket.

Theologians could possibly rationalize this. They, who disagree amongst themselves on so many facets of religion, do however agree quite unanimously on one main fact. They agree that Jesus came into the world *'in the fullness of time'*. They agree that there never was a more opportune time, in the history of the world, for the advent of the Son of God, than two millenniums ago. His coming was perfectly timed. The Greek thinkers were becoming more and more disillusioned by their Mount Olympus Gods. They were beginning to search for a new God. The Romans had built a web of straight roads throughout Europe that were ready to carry the message of His coming. But as one reviews the history of the world, one begins to realise that there is nothing peculiar about this. All great inventions and all great world movements have come about in the *'fullness of time'*. Wood was found in plenty to feed the early hunger pangs of steam. Coal was discovered in time to prevent the country being denuded of its trees. Electricity came in time to use the newly discovered coal and oil. The atom was split. All these great gifts of nature had been there, in hiding, since the beginning to time; but the blindfold was not removed from man's eyes, for him to see them, until … 'the fullness of time'.

I am an Anglican priest. If I had been asked to preach a sermon about the privies of Wales and not write a book about them, I think I would use the leisurely, slowly creeping, entrance of the water closet into our civilisation, as another wonderful example of how God's gifts are given to us when we are most ready to enjoy them. And I would say, in my sermon, that I could not imagine how any good historian could ever be an atheist. An honest historian surely must postulate for himself a Creator and a Planner; and an immensely intelligent Creator and Planner at that. A Creator who has planted His gifts to mankind since the beginning of time and unwraps them one by one, but only … 'in the fullness of time'.

How awful if the order of things had been changed and inventions and innovations were born before their time. If television had been invented two hundred years ago, S4C would have been paid fat advertising fees by the *Times* newspaper for promoting the fact that its newspaper sheets, cut into small squares, provided far softer wipes for the nether end than either tufts of grass, or moss, or soft stones.

Amazingly, enough sanitary discoveries were made throughout the centuries, and they were put into isolated use. There was an early water system in 1169 in the Palace of Westminster. By the late 16th Century large households began to have indoor fountains, and indoor baths, and indoor toilets. Inventors and science boffins had been working for centuries on the possibility of having nice, clean, non-smelly, inside toilets for all. Sir John Harrington, godson of Queen Elizabeth I, is reputed to have devised a water closet where the water from the cistern placed above the seat would flush the contents of the pan away in one flush, very much like the system we have today. He even wrote the first Book of Privies and called it *'Metamorphis of Ajax'*. The Queen had one of her godson's inventions installed in Richmond Palace and no doubt enjoyed its rich benefits. But for others it was not to be. Sir John Harrington, like all his inventor friends, was told very firmly: "The world is not yet ready for your ideas. It is not yet the fullness of time for a pull chain indoor water closet."

III

Mirror, Mirror on the Wall ...

꧁

The finest lavatory in England is reputed to be the one at Hampden Manor, Kidlington, Oxfordshire. And so it should be, it was designed by the same wonderful architect, Sir John Vanbrugh, who built the beautiful Blenheim Palace. The work on the palace was completed in 1715. Whist the work was going on Sir John stayed at Hampden Manor nearby. His host was most helpful, supplying most of the farm carts, horses and men used in the building at Blenheim. Sir John was so grateful to him, both for his hospitality and his help with the Palace construction, that he promised to build him, as a gift, "the finest lavatory in the whole of England and a water one t'boot".

One has to admit that the Hampden Manor privy is a truly elegant one and it still stands proud today. It could claim to be the finest, and the most elegant, and the handsomest loo in England ... but not in all Britain. I think the fairest and the most elegant privy I have ever seen anywhere is the Abercamlais Dovecote Privy in Brecon. Abercamlais is an amazing house. In 1537 a very famous vicar called "Y Ficar Gwyn" (the White Vicar), moved into this lovely old mansion and since that time all the owners of the house, ten generations of them, have been priests in holy orders; all except one, Thomas Williams, who was High Sheriff in his day and died in 1700.

The Camlais is a little rivulet that flows into the larger River Usk. The

Built to be "the finest closet in England". Hampden Manor kidlinston

beautiful Dovecote Privy belonging to the house was built astride the Camlais somewhere around the year 1700; a little earlier than the "finest privy in England" created in Kidlington. It has two separate entrances. The gentlemen of the house went down the front path and through the eastern door; the servants would come out of the backdoor of the house, and, using a plank to cross the river, would enter by the north door. It appears that there was a sort of hessian curtain separating the gentlemen from the servants.

Historians are not certain which of the owners of Abercamlais built this wonderful edifice, but apparently the motive for its creation was not as noble as that of its English counterpart. The Hampden Manor Privy was built as a loving gift from a grateful architect to his host. I regret to say that the Abercamlais Privy

Abercamlais Dovecote-Privy
"The finest in all Britain"

was built because of pride and envy. The family had split into two. There was the Abercamlais branch and the Penport branch; both occupying their own grand houses close to each other. Over the years, the two families got on well together and at times they even intermarried. But there were also periods of strained relations.

The Dovecote Privy was built during one of these "strained relations" periods. A time of rivalry. It was built as something the Penport family would envy; something that was far more elegant than any privy they might ever possess. As a clergyman, I fail to see how historians plead ignorance to the name of the owner that designed this lovely edifice. It has to be the High Sheriff Thomas Williams, the only owner who was not a clergyman, and who died in 1700. For be ye well assured that no clerk in Holy Orders would have been capable of nurturing, within himself, sufficient sinful pride and envy to carry out such a task! But I am still grateful to him for building such a lovely Privy.

IV

Privy Pioneers

❧

To meet the first discoverer of the indoor toilet you have to travel to Knossos on the Island of Crete. There lived on this Island five thousand years before Christ was born, [some say 7,000 years BC] a strange and ultra intelligent people. When excavations began on the Island in the early 1900s it was the Knossos of the later Minoan period that surfaced. So it is of the period of 1,700 BC that we look for evidence of their plumbing and other abilities.

Parts of the King's Palace have been excavated and reconstructed so that today, they appear very much as they did 3,700 years ago. The reconstructed palace looks far more modern than does Penrhyn Castle, in Llandegai, that was built in 1820. It had four stories and 1,500 rooms. The drainage system consisted of terra-cota pipes, from 4"-6" in diameter. The pipes had perfect socket joints, so ta-

Palace of Minos, circa 1,700 BC

pered that the narrow end of the pipe fitted tightly into the broad end of the other. The tapering sections allowed for a jetting action to prevent the accumulation of sediment. (This perhaps is something that we, today, could try). The drainage pipes were all laid under the passages and not under the living quarters. Archaeologists found that some of the main sewers still carried away surface water from the site. The Queen's bathtub was found intact in her room. It is made of terra-cotta, and decorated in a bass relief of a watery motif of reeds. It was evidently filled and emptied by hand but the used water was discarded into a cavity in the floor connected directly to the main sewer. [It was far more modern than the zinc one my mother bathed me in on Friday nights]. The drainage system was connected to the river Kairatos.

Not far away we find the earliest "flushing" water closet in the world. It was flushed by rainwater in the winter and by water held in cisterns in the dry summer. There were several other closets found in the palace. The Minoans of Knossos were enjoying a plumbing system similar to that enjoyed in our country during mid-Victorian times, and all this was happening over 1,000 years before Rome was born as a new city on the Tiber.

Frescos on the walls show Minoan women dressed in long last century type cotton dresses, the kind that I remember my mother wearing on summer days. It was thought at first that these extraordinary people enjoyed bull fighting, but further study of the wall frescos showed that these cultured, intelligent, Minoans had no place for such a cruel, dastardly, sport. Their hobby was "bull leaping" which was much more fun both for the womenfolk and for the bull. The woman would wave a rag at the bull; the bull would lower its head and charge, the woman would drop the cloth; grab the bull by the horns, the bull would toss the woman over its head; she would somersault into the air and make a good landing on both feet behind the bull.

These are a people whose life on earth intrigues me. No one seems to know where they came from in those dark early days. There was not even an Egyptian civilisation when they first made their appearance in Crete. The only other flicker of intelligent life had just been lit in China. It appears, too, that the Minoan dynasty came to an end a few centuries before the birth of Christ; just as suddenly, and just as mysteriously, as it had come about. No one seems to know why it disappeared. Some say it must have been an earthquake, others that they were killed in battle. But Knossos was a city of 100,000 people in its hey day all living within an area of about 22 acres. I remember asking the Professor of Archaeology from Heraklion University if he had any idea where these people had come from. He just shrugged his shoulders. I pointed up to the planets above and he retorted: "Your guess is just as good as anyone else's."

The Queen's bath, Knossos 1,700 BC

Now having said all that about an ancient people whose culture and way of life intrigue me I now say that it was the Minoans, and not the Romans, or the Greeks, or the Egyptians, who were the first to invent an indoor loo. Unfortunately they left suddenly, or were killed, before they could show others how it was done.

Someone has said—and if I know anything about Universities—has received a Ph.D. for saying it, that human beings excrete ten per cent of all they eat. If this body waste is not disposed of quickly it becomes a problem—a problem that has exercised the mind of mankind since the beginning of time.

It has often been suggested that it was the Romans who pioneered the idea of Water Closets. Many have also ventured the opinion that the Romans must have been shocked to see how backward the Ancient Britons were, and particularly the way the Celts would just crouch down and do their business whenever and wherever they felt like it. I have never felt happy with either of these statements.

There is no denying that the Romans did build, for their armies, good solid, water toilets, and baths. They became congenial meeting places for the men and they were encouraged to use them as clubrooms and social meeting places. But I have always had the feeling that this enthusiasm for lavatorial hygiene was a military exercise confined to the army. Rome found that more men died of typhoid and cholera and other water borne diseases than were lost in the fighting. This was not only in Britain but throughout their campaigns in Europe. So, in order to reduce causalities, hygienic toilets were built. Remains of these have been found at Chester, and at Caernarfon, and more recently at Caerleon. The soldiers that manned Hadrian's Wall were also supplied with four-star soldier conveniences. But it is also true to say that very few of all the Roman villas that civilian Romans built for their retirement (if indeed any) have been found to have had a covered closet like the military convenience. A good number of these Roman villas were recently excavated in Winchester and I think I am right in saying that not one of them had a separate loo. For the rich retired Roman Centurion and his wife, when the call came it would be, "Left, Right," to the bottom of the garden hole. Possibly a posher and a bigger hole than that of the conquered Briton, but a garden hole nevertheless. It would be a case of:- "When in Britain do as the Britons do".

I am not quite sure whether I can go along with this idea that the old Briton was as backward as he was made out to be. He would have had a good relationship with Phoenician traders long before he had ever met a Roman. It was from the Phoenician and the Eastern Church that the Celts received the Christian Gospel. He could have taught his Roman conqueror a thing or two about the Christian religion and probably did. There was a bishop and a cathedral in Bangor 50 years before Rome's first official missionary St Augustine was born. The Celts observed Easter the same week as the Eastern Orthodox Church and not the Roman date. The Celtic monks had their hair tonsured in the Eastern and not in the Roman fashion. We were not entirely dependent on Roman culture even as Ancient Britons!

The latrines at Prysg Roman Fort in Caerleon, Mon. The Prysg Roman Fort.

We do tend, possibly, to think of the conquering army as being made up of rich Roman patriarchs. The officers might have been, but the ordinary soldiers were to a great extent conscripts from Spain and France and other conquered countries. Our British lavatorial customs would not have shocked these young men one little bit. When they went home on leave to Spain and France and Greece they quite happily went to the bottom of the garden and dug a hole just like the Celts did in Britain. Even today some of our European neighbours haven't managed even to catch up with us in matters lavatorial. Those who like myself have felt the call of nature in Greece, and who have had to stand, legs apart, over a Greek public convenience will know what I mean.

The man who led II Augusta Legion into Britain later became the Emperor Vespasian. When the legion was moved to Caerleon, building a latrine for the soldiers became a top priority. The Prysg Latrine has been recently excavated with its complicated sewage system. And yet we know that almost at the same time that the Prysg Latrines were built for the military in Britain, the streets and pavements of Rome were lined with buckets, and chamber pots, and commodes, for the use of civilians—plebeians and patriarchs alike. We know this because one of the first acts of Vespasian, after being crowned emperor, was to sell, to the highest bidder, the right to collect and to re-sell the pavement bucket contents. This would then be used by the clothing trade. Vespasian, we are told, was the son of a money-lender.

Hywel Dda, nearly a thousand years later, had exactly the same idea as the Roman Emperor. He also found that there was brass in muck and laid down in his laws that every community should appoint a sort of minister of urine or "Bismaer", "Dung Mayor", to arrange for the selling of its human excrement. The term mayor was possibly a little derisory, but the holder was still regarded as a person of some importance. It is interesting to note that Hywel Dda in his Laws describes the privy by its more dignified name of 'Y Ty Bychan'.

Throughout the Roman occupation, and after the departure of the Roman Legions, the Christian monks kept up their own standard of hygiene. Some of the monastic closets were as cleverly constructed as were those of the Roman garrisons. But they were all dependent on their being sited over a fast flowing stream.

Then came the Norman conquerors. They taught us how to build castles and great cathedrals with beautiful arches. They hadn't got a clue on how to build privies. They built rows of niches high up in the castle

The twelve 'garderobes' along the walls of Conwy Castle

walls over a hole in the wall. Townspeople and possibly soldiers too, would sit on seats in the niches and perform. This allowed the excrements of hundreds of people to trickle its way down the castle wall into the moat below, which became a stagnant sewer. These insanitary inventions were known by the most distinguished name of *'garderobes'*.

Minoans, Romans, Normans, Christian Monks, all played their part, but in Britain, the real pioneers, men like Cummings, Moule, Bramah, and Crapper were yet to come many centuries later.

V

The Cesspit Fill

I recently read the report of archaeologist Kenneth Murphy, and his team, "The Bulletin of the Board of Celtic Studies" Vol.XXXVI 1989. I was asked, by CADW to research the history of the Privies of Wales. He, poor chap, was asked by the National Trust, as leader of the Dyfed Archaeological Society, to examine the contents of the cesspit, of the Tudor Merchants House, Tenby, Dyfed. I only wish I could have made my research sound as fascinating as his.

The Tudor Merchant's House stands in Quay Street, Tenby, Dyfed. The house is 16th Century and was carefully and lovingly restored by the National Trust in 1939. The cesspit was found under the floor of the Latrine Tower. It measured 1.5m x 1m and was 1.3m deep. Not very big for such a large, three floored, building. As it was indoors it must have promulgated a most awful pong throughout the house. And to make matters worse it was situated near the kitchens and the family eating quarters.

Dr Murphy, and his team, carefully extracted the contents. They were sieved through extra fine sieves; examined through extra powerful microscopes. Fruit stones, and cereal seeds, were found in plenty. It became clear that the people of 500 years ago took as much care of their diet as do people today.

A great number of Prunus Domestica (Prunes and Custard, for you know what) were found. Raspberries, blackberries, and strawberries ac-

The Tudor Merchant's House, Tenby

counted for much of the diet. The evidence of utilatissimum L, flax and hemp, could also suggest a conscious effort to consume roughage.

Interestingly the cesspool also contained small pieces of woven material. It must be more than a coincidence that hemp, and Irish linen, were

41

recorded as regular imports into the port of Tenby during this period. There is little doubt that these, and the sheep's wool recovered, could have been the remains of 'toilet paper' and sanitary towels. Judging by the contents of the privy it is also quite evident that there must have been a good deal of ale making and ale drinking in Tenby, 500 years ago. I learned all this from the report of Sandra Nye, who was a member of the team.

Another report is by John Phipps. He seems to specialise in the 'mineralised insect remains'. The other day a friend of mine was waxing strong about the wonders of the Computer and its Web. I had just read John Phipps's "Fly Paparia Report", so I said to him:- "That's nothing mate, there's a chap called John Phipps—an archaeologist—and he has been able to analyse, from the mineralised remains of insects, that the flies that died in a cesspool, in the 15th Century, were without a doubt the Ephydrid Fly, Teichomyza Fusuca Macquart, that is still around to-day and its favourite diet, to this day, is human faeces and urine."

Jane Evans, another member of the team, has also been able to iden-tify the different kinds of fish that would have adorned the rich man's table in the reign of Queen Elizabeth 1 (I quote all this to show what a great loss it is to science that our old privies are being demolished). The fish would have been, herring, common eel, mullet, plaice, skate/ray, cod, shark, and bass.

I found Andrew Jones, and his colleague's, "Parasitological Investiga-tion", most intriguing. These men were able to say with confidence that the cesspool contents were loaded with samples of trichuris ova. They even counted the trichuris ova as 3,900 per gramme deposit. They go as far as to say that there were two different species of this particular ova in the Tenby cesspool. These ovas are usually identified with whipworms. Light infestation of whip worm apparently may cause little harm to the host, but a heavy worm burden can cause diarrhoea, blood in the faeces, and prolapse of the rectum. It can also stunt children's growth. These scientists even measured the ova. They were 49.7 microns long and 25.5

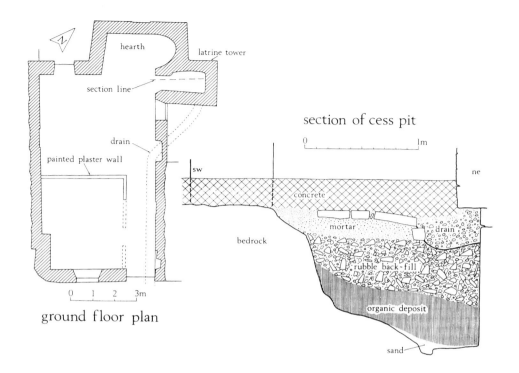

hearth

latrine tower

section line

section of cess pit

0   1m

drain

painted plaster wall

sw

ne

concrete

mortar

drain

bedrock

rubble back-fill

0   1   2   3m

organic deposit

ground floor plan

sand

microns wide (no figure is given for body diameter). It appears that the trichuris is very particular where he lives. He will only set up home in the intestines of men and pigs. No other mammals will do.

The parasitological team also discovered that the Elizabethan gentleman nurtured, inside him, another parasite predator—the large roundworm—or the Ascaris. This worm is also peculiar to pigs and humans.

I had, of course always known that cats and dogs and horses and all domestic animals had to be regularly wormed. But humans! I began to wonder if my little grandchildren's tummies were full of wriggling worms.

It was then I remembered something that I had long forgotten, or had consciously pushed into my deep unconscious, because it was too unworthy to be remembered. I was wormed when I was a child. I am 82 years of age and I was wormed every Friday night throughout my childhood days. I can even remember the name of the evil smelling, evil tasting, medication that was used—it was asseopheata. There was a less violent de-wormer made of wormwood.

Friday night was bath night. The zinc bath was brought in front of a roaring fire. As soon as I had been dried with a warm towel my mother would produce two medicine bottles. One dessert spoonful of Syrup of Figs was given, under mild protest, to combat constipation, whatever the condition the bowels were at the time of taking. But the other—the asseopheata! There was crying and there were tantrums, over the spoonful of asseopheta. But in the end common sense prevailed.

Mothers described to their children the horror of the worms that eat away at your intestines—they were called tape worms and ring worms—they were always waiting for the food you eat to descend from your mouth to your tummy—especially sweets. Apparently, if not killed off with asseopheta , they would become so many that they would demand all the food you eat, leaving nothing for your body growth. They would leave you pale and weakly and very often you could end up a midget. When a child looked pale and puny the first question asked was "Has he got worms?" I even remember the Welsh word we used for worms "llyngir", "Oes ganddo fo lyngir?".

Mothers on Friday nights would re-tell the story of Mary Lisa. It was found that Mary Lisa had a tape worm inside her tummy. It had grown so large that even asseopheata couldn't kill it. It was eating all her food so that Mary Lisa was getting smaller and smaller and the nasty tape worm inside her was becoming bigger and bigger.

The doctor ordered her mother to boil a quart of milk and place it in a large basin. Mary Lisa was to lie with her head over the basin and inhale the vapours of the rich creamy milk.

In minutes, Mary Lisa's father and mother and the doctor saw a large flat, worm nearly as large as a snake coming out of her mouth and direct itself towards the milk. The doctor took his knife and killed it and from that day onwards, Mary Lisa began to grow again into a strong, healthy girl.

I then began to wonder if this sort of thing, that happened in my childhood days, still went on, and if not, when did it stop? What was the name of the doctor, or the pharmacist who discovered the cure?

I asked my G.P. He told me that worms have not been completely eradicated. They still exist inside many children and some adults too. But he did add that archaeologists of the future would find far less evidence of it than did the Tenby team. But as a parting shot he did say to me:-

"It is always worth having a little look in the pan, every now and again, before you pull the plug, just in case. If there are any there, they will be little bits like thin spaghetti, and they will be wiggling their bottoms at you."

VI

History
1850 to 1950
❧

For many centuries the whole of Britain persevered with its earth privies and its gongfermors, and its night carts, and its ladies in crinoline dresses walking up the garden to "pick a rose", and ending up with having to use a wet spade to shovel mud into the holes they had just vacated. Towns still rang out to the cries of 'garde l'eau'.

Around the year 1850 the situation changed a little for the better with the advent of the bucket privy. It is so difficult to believe that no one thought of the simple bucket until the turn of the century. Queen Victoria was dead before the first privy bucket began to overtake the earth privy. All this was because there was a stubbornness amongst the people, and amongst politicians, against change. By the beginning of the 20th Century our state of hygiene, as a nation, had become appalling. This would be particularly true of the industrial areas in South Wales that, like the Midlands, attracted armies of urban workers flocking to earn the fabled wealth of the coalmines.

In the industrial parts of Wales as many as 30 people would share a single privy. Health reports state that 28% of children died before the age of five, mostly of typhoid and cholera, and other water carried illnesses. Years of using the same earth cesspool, originally built too near to the larger houses, was beginning to exact its toll. The cesspit liquid penetrated under the foundation of the houses and the poisonous odour, and the gasses it emitted affected the health of the 'downstairs' servants.

Good example of early bucket type

The land stank of excrement. People's bodies stank of it. They carried it on their shoes and on their clothes into their homes. Noble judges, who sat in judgement over them, waved posies of lavender and other herbs under their noses to dissipate the smell. The whole country seemed to be heading for the same fate that befell the aforesaid gongfermor Richard Raker, the man, who in 1326, met with a dreadful death when he fell through the rotten planks of his homemade privy and "drowned monstrously in his own excrement".

But throughout this period there were inventors and men of science, experimenting and hoping to discover the closet that would be acceptable to the people and that would put an end to their misery. But strangely their efforts were not welcome. Neither government, nor people, wanted changes made in the ways the populace eased itself. Politicians were afraid that the eventual solution, based on the use of water, would cause a financial crisis. Such a discovery could also denude the country of its drinking water. It would most certainly mean constructing a new network of water sewers at great cost.

But strangely ordinary little families were also most antagonistic to change; they were not for turning. From the 1850s onwards the earth garden privy had started to give place to the bucket privy. The bucket privy was so much cleaner, the buckets had lids that made them less of a target for rats and flies and smells. With just a bucket to house and not a deep smelly trench, it was so much easier to concentrate on the little building itself. So the new bucket privies began to have walls and a roof. They had little doors that shut and even a little niche in the wall to hold a candle or a lantern for nocturnal users. The new bucket privy had transformed itself into a little quiet place apart in a world that was becoming unrestful and overcrowded. People were saying, "This is enough We are now a happy people".

My church records in Llandegai tell me that its little "two-down one-up" little cottages were more often that not occupied by large families. There would be father and mother and seven or eight children and very often a grandmother to boot. Father and mother and the baby would occupy the downstairs 'siambar', the boys would climb the ladder to the loft. The main article of furniture, the Welsh dresser, doubled up as a room divider and grandma and the girls would bed down on straw pallets behind the dresser in the living room. The 'Ty Bach' had become more than a place of easement for members of the family, and especially I would think, for the mother. It was a little place apart where she could be alone, where she could enjoy a little 'space' if only for a few minutes of the day. There was now, understandably, a deep prejudice against anything that would remove this place of calm from the busy, hurly burly life of bringing up children. There was a fear that a newly invented water contraption inside the house could take that small centre of tranquillity away for ever.

And there was another reason too. It might sound trivial to many of us today, but our forbears, a good many of them, could not afford the luxury of having their excrement carried away from their property. When a man had a small garden and six hungry children it was a necessity.

Garden soil has to be fed, and garden soil that has to grow potatoes one year after another has to be very well fed. The stuff that these gardens grew was strictly organic the head of the household could not afford any other.

Summer to us living in Blaenau Ffestiniog was when the new potatoes' seller's horse and cart arrived from Morfa Bychan. The herald of warmer weather to come, would ring a bell and cry out *"Tatws Morfa Bychan, Tatws Morfa Bychan"*. No potatoes ever tasted as good as Tatws Morfa Bychan and every single one of them had been organically grown.

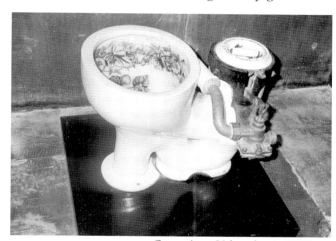

Cummings Valve closet, 1775

The government and its people, for differing reasons, could turn a blind eye on the lack of hygiene, and its accompanying odours, but Local Authorities couldn't. The illnesses and the early deaths, were laid at their door. Parliament enacted one Health Act after another knowing that they would be ignored. The 1848 act stated that a fixed sanitary arrangement of some kind whether ash closet, or water closet, or bucket, must be fitted to every household. Local Authorities began to organise competitions for the best designed watercloset. There was one famous competition at the International Exhibition of Hygiene in South Kensington in 1884. There were 33 entries. Marks were given for the shape of the privy and for its general comfort. Each privy was then submitted to the same test. Into each pan was placed 10 small potatoes, some sponge, and four thin sheets of paper, and it was necessary that all be removed at the one flushing. Only three passed the test successfully.

But in spite of prejudice there were a few boffins who kept on working to clean up the whole system. As early as 1596 Sir John Harrington invented an indoor closet. But it seems that the only person who bought one was his godmother Queen Elizabeth. She had it installed in Richmond Castle and, as far as we know, it worked well. But no one else wanted to know about this new fangled invention.

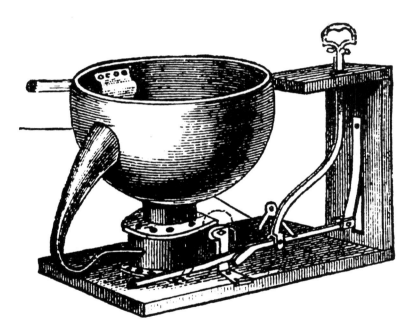

What a Bramah! A Joseph Bramah's valve closet, 1778

The main problem was that although the new water closet allowed the pan to be flushed during its emptying period, it back carried all kinds of bad odours to the house from the sewer or cesspool below.

50

Andrew Cummings, a watch maker, in 1775, was the first man to apply for patent rights on a water closet. He invented the 'S' bend pan, that allowed static water to remain in the pan after flushing to act as a guard or a valve, that prevented rising odours and gasses.

The Cummings model was greatly improved, three years later, by a man called Joseph Bramah. He invented the hinged valve inside the cistern that controlled the flow of water. This meant that after every usage only a measured amount of water needed to be used to flush and keep the pan clean. The Bramah hinged valve was such a wonderful invention that for a time it added a new word into the English language. Anything that today would be described as 'super' or 'cool', was then described as 'bramah' and this went on until about the 1920s. By 1797 Joseph Bramah had sold and installed 6,000 Bramah Closets in Britain. There is no doubt that this man set the trend for the next hundred years for those who could afford to pay his price.

But there was no rejoicing amongst those who were living in more rural parts of Britain, and of Wales in particular. These were the those who were without hope of having piped water. Drinking water very often had to be carried across fields in buckets. The content of these buckets was much too precious to be used to flush Bramah's or anyone else's toilet. It was for this reason that the earth toilet boffins continued their experimentation. Throughout the period, earth closet engineers were working alongside their water closet colleagues.

A Parker after Moule Indoor Earth Closet

51

It comes at no great surprise to me that the most ingenious of these was a person of similar vocation to myself. He was the Reverend Henry Moule. His invention, in 1860, enabled the earth privy idea to be efficiently used inside the house.

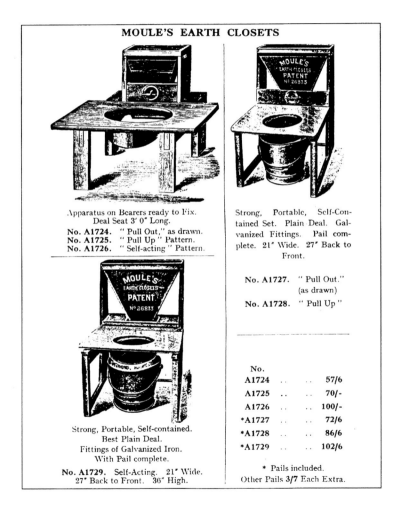

MOULE'S EARTH CLOSETS

Apparatus on Bearers ready to Fix.
Deal Seat 3' 0" Long.
No. A1724. " Pull Out," as drawn.
No. A1725. " Pull Up " Pattern.
No. A1726. " Self-acting " Pattern.

Strong, Portable, Self-contained.
Best Plain Deal.
Fittings of Galvanized Iron.
With Pail complete.
No. A1729. Self-Acting. 21" Wide.
27" Back to Front. 36" High.

Strong, Portable, Self-Contained Set. Plain Deal. Galvanized Fittings. Pail complete. 21" Wide. 27" Back to Front.

No. A1727. " Pull Out."
(as drawn)
No. A1728. " Pull Up "

No.			
A1724	..	..	57/6
A1725	..	..	70/-
A1726	..	..	100/-
*A1727	..	..	72/6
*A1728	..	..	86/6
*A1729	..	..	102/6

* Pails included.
Other Pails **3/7** Each Extra.

The old earth privies had gone out of fashion because they were smelly, they attracted flies and rats, and more than anything else they were so difficult to use. The soil, used to reduce the odours, was housed outside the privy. During the winter this was often reduced to a muddy heap.

The Moule Closet, however, was a great success. It was fitted with a cistern that contained a quantity of dry soil. After using the toilet the user would pull a little lever at the side and a measured amount of soil would pour into the bucket beneath. It was a great boon for the ladies. They sold in their thousands all over the world. They were installed in factories, schools, barracks and prisons. Wakefield jail had 776 fitted. Amazingly enough sales continued until the outbreak of World War II (see sales catalogue page opposite). They cost £5 2s 6p in 1936 and this included the price of the bucket. They were efficient. But, nevertheless, contents had still to be emptied manually, and there was also the regular chore of having to grind down the soil and keeping it dry.

Bramah with his water closet for urban dwellers, and Moule with his earth closet for the rural populace, kept the menace of a universal in-door loo at bay until very nearly the middle of the 20th Century.

Canon Wynzie Richard reminded me of how Mrs Betty Miller (nee Thomas) of the Old Quarry Lampeter, brought her two small children from their home in the United States to see the country where their mummy had been brought up. This was in the 1950s. They were visiting a cottage in Cwmann, when Betsan, the little girl, decided she wanted to spend a penny. She was dispatched to the privy at the bottom of the garden. Soon there was a shout to her brother from below, "Oi!, Louis, come and see this quaint little cabin that the people in the cottage call their bathroom". Louis is now a High Court Judge and Betsan a very successful lawyer in the USA. Mrs Sylvia Woollam of Llannon tells me that when she left home to get married in the 1960s the old home still used an outside privy, and she tells me too that there is a working privy, in daily use, not far from her present home but she feels it wiser not to disclose its location just in case the authorities decide to close it down.

But this little privy must be the exception, because all bottom of the garden privies in Britain were made redundant in the 1950s and 1960s and we have been burying them every since.

The campaign for an Indoor Water Closet had eventually won the day. Its great champions were Alexander Cummings, the watch maker, and Joseph Bramah, the perfectionist, and Henry Moule, the parson. But they were mere heralds of a greater that was to come. If you take the lid off even the most modern of lavatory cisterns and peep inside you will be looking at the great invention known as the "Silent Valveless Water Waste Preventer" that has been but little improved upon over the years. You will have been looking at the ingenious invention of Thomas Crapper who, in the latter half of the 19th Century, became the Elvis Presley of plumbing.

VII

The Penrhyn Charade

In the early 1800s Richard Douglas Pennant, of Penrhyn, Bangor set about building an elegant castle for himself. A beautiful Elizabethan mansion house, that had been home to the Penrhyn family for centuries was pulled down, and the foundations of a pseudo Norman Castle were laid on the site where it had stood.

The fine oak panelling at Penrhyn

The third richest man in Britain changed the course of the river, so that it would run through his park; and built a seven mile wall so that he could live an undisturbed life within his new domain. And to be quite honest it was a very hard earned domain. Richard Pennant, the aristocrat, was also one of the greatest entrepreneurs of his day. The new barons of industry in the Midlands, were proud to shake his hand and to accept his advice.

In his day, and for the next 120 years, children wrote not on paper, but with a slate pencil on writing slates that had a wooden frames. These slate pencils and framed slates, were made in a factory in Switzerland. The Swiss factory had the monopoly of making them for all the schools in the world. Whether Richard Pennant travelled to Switzerland and saw the slate pencils and the slate writing pads being made, or whether a friend brought a sample back for him to see, we don't know. But the sight of the writing slate and the slate pencil was enough for our great industrialist. Within weeks the man who owned his own slate quarry and had his own forestry, had built workshops in Llandegai for the production of thousands of writing slates and pencils. Within three years the Swiss firm that had had the world monopoly had to close its doors. The Pennant factory, in Llandegai, had by now gained a world monopoly.

Whilst the castle was being built, London agents were told to buy the best paintings, and the best of furniture, and silverware, and crockery, that money could buy. The aristocrat/industrialist was determined to have only the best for himself.

When the Castle was completed there is no doubt that there were parties and castle warming banquets held regularly. The squire would be anxious to show off his vast new acquisition. The constant frou frou of ladies crinoline dresses could be heard along its corridors and men in wigs and tail coated suits, sat at its tables.

During a banquet the huge oak tables would sag under the weight of the heavy silverware displaying huge joints of every kind of meat, and

Behind the potty cupboard

bird, and fish. Casks of ale would have been carried into the vast Dining Hall to quench the guests' thirst. Gallons upon gallons of ale would be consumed at every banquet. When the eating and the ale drinking was done it was the custom, as it often is today, for the host to call for silence. He would say:- "Possibly the ladies would like to retire to the lounge, and leave the gentlemen to their port". The ladies would dutifully rise and follow their hostess to the Grand Hall. As soon as the last of them had disappeared a servant would quickly and quietly, shut the door and the male guests would stampede; not, as one would imagine, to the port, but to the chamber pot cupboard cunningly hidden in the oak panelling. The male guests, with bladders bloated with ale, would have sat cross legged waiting for the host's bidding to the ladies.

The castle was built after 1820. That really is not such a long time ago. If I had been born of a nobler breed, my great-grandfather could have been amongst those stampeding to use the potty. I have often wondered if the ladies knew what was going on in the dining room once they had withdrawn. Had a single husband had the courage to grass to his wife the secret of the chamber pot cupboard, and would she, shielding her mouth behind her fan, have repeated it to the others?

This was the period when earth privies were giving place to bucket privies. Penrhyn was not the only great mansion to have a hidden chamber cupboard, but it probably was amongst the last to be installed. The Reverend Moule had sold thousands of his automatic earth models 50 years before the castle was built, Bramah Loos were all the go years earlier. What I find strange is that this business entrepreneur at Penrhyn Castle should have been so old fashioned as to require his guests, staying in his posh new castle, to use old world potties.

VIII

The Making of
a Privy

❧

R.P. Jones of Llangernyw, Conwy, is able to describe the making of a garden privy. He says that as the new house was being built all the surplus material would be set apart; the odd bits of wood, broken slates, and bricks that were a bit uneven.

The site of the privy, in the garden, would have been chosen just as carefully as had been the site of the house itself. The direction of the wind would also have been noted in the metrological science of the day.

Surplus materials would have been carried to the designated site of the *Ty-Bach*. When the house had been completed, the brickie/joiner would start work on the edifice, the foundations, then walls, and the roofing. Then would come the day when the bricklayer would knock on the kitchen door of the newly built house and ask to see the "mistress". With eyes cast downwards in deference to the sensitivity of the architectural planning ahead, he would ask his lady-client the inevitable: "Um, er, cough, … we need to know, Ma'am, whether you wish one, two or three holed lavatory seats?"

"One I think, Mr. Cadwaladr", would come the shy retort. "There is only Mr. Pughe and myself". There would be a knowing nod from Mr. Cadwaladr.

A lavatory seat, its shape, and the number of holes in it, can tell the historian nearly as much about the families that used these old privies as the cess pit contents can tell the archaeologist.

A young family three-seater

Mr and Mrs Pughe were probably both middle aged and by now both rather on the portly side and able to fit into the same size hole as each other. One hole would do nicely for the two of them. The broad village blacksmith with his new bride, and baby, on the other hand, would order a three seater. The larger hole would be for himself, the smaller for his youngish wasp waisted new bride, and the third seat, lower and small enough to accommodate a potty, would be for the baby or the baby that was yet to come.

I have read many books on privies and many of them try to purvey to us that sentimental tosh about the cosiness of the little family, father, and mother, and baby, going to the loo together to have their little time apart. That of course is absolute rubbish. The three seaters were never meant, nor were they used, for communal sittings. There were three seats. The larger was for father and the boys as they grew up would graduate into it. The smaller was for mum and the girls, the tiny little hole was for baby and all the other many babies that would want to use it in the future. Normally the only time when this loo accommodated more than one person would be when the mother and baby would go in together for a quiet potty training session whilst dad was at work, and the other children were in school. It could be, too, that two of the girls would sit together and have a little giggle. But the very idea of mum and dad and the baby going together, at regular intervals every day, is so illogical. My parish registers tell me that houses with babies, during this period were also houses cram packed with children. One has to ask if it is true that mum and dad went to the loo together and took baby Joseph with them, who would be left in the house to look after little Benjamin and his many brothers?

No! the three-holer was made to accommodate a growing family— but one at a time. And yet I am always ready to learn. Mrs Megan Thomas of Sketty tells me that she was one of 13 children. For such a large family a 'one per session turn' was not always possible. She also tells me that if one of the little ones wanted to go, especially in the evenings, they would have to be accompanied by one of the grown up sisters. So the tendency was to gather all the little ones together and tell them that Mary wanted to go to the loo so they had all better go as well. Incidentally, the old privy at Cwm Terrace, that had served its large family of 15 for many years, became an air raid causality in 1942. There must have been thousands of them bombed during the war, but this is the first for me to hear of, so I feel I must record it.

Something like that used to happen in our home of six children. When the car was nearly packed for holiday or a long run, mum would give the order, "Now everybody off to spend a penny". There were cries of

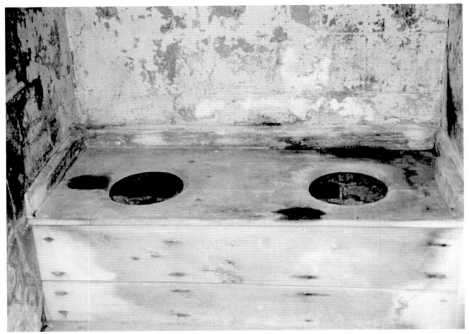

Two equi-holer economy—for a large family

"Don't want to" or "I've only just been". But it was never a request it was a command—and they went.

The two equal-sized hole bucket loo, however, was built especially for a grown family—mum and dad and four or five hefty lads. The privy would be used by the large family one bucket at a time. Sunday till Wednesday, it was understood that all were to use left-hand facing bucket. Mid-week father would make his survey. If he felt it necessary he would close down the left-hand facing by putting the lid over it. The message would be understood that from now until the end of the week when the buckets would be emptied, that only the right-hand facing bucket would be used. In this way father would be able to make a once weekly two bucket journey, and know before he began his walk that neither bucket exceeded the safety level. Often however, father would delegate authority to other members of the family.

their garden privy. For years, after it had ceased to be a privy, their now grown-up daughters had used it as a super Wendy House. There had been odd times when it has served as a 'shop' and as a 'hospital' and on one occasion, when one of the smaller girls had a crush on the vicar, as a 'church'. Angharad, when she was eight years old, had taken ages hand-sewing curtains for one of its windows.

In the same mail-bag following the advertising of my research into Welsh privies, a lovely lady, Leri Roberts, from Porthmadog, wrote to say that her redundant Ty Bach—her Privy—used to double as a hospital and as a zoo! The hospital bit was where injured animals and pregnant pet rabbits would be housed. But a *zoo*!? The only creature which lived in her zoo, apparently, was a huge spider that she had become very fond of. She would hurry home from school and make straight for the old privy and catch flies to place in her pet spider's web. She had come to believe that her spider knew her because he would always await her arrival home; sitting there legs and arms waving at her (but probably just licking his lips in anticipation of a lazy spider's tea) at the same time every day. He'd almost eat her dead-fly offering from the palm of her hand. She also remembers becoming obsessed with the idea that her spider would die if she was not around to feed him.

Without a doubt all privies became natural habitats for a variety of insects, and rats, and other uninvited guests. Mrs Megan Jones, of Dolgellau, told me a wonderful tale of her experience as a new bride visiting her in-laws. She wrote:

"I am married to a farmer's son, but my husband is not a farmer. The year we were married his parents invited us to spend Christmas with them on the farm. We had goose for Christmas dinner, deliciously cooked on the Aga, and I'm afraid I overdid things a little. In the middle of the night I had the most awful collywobbles and had to take the dreaded path to the garden privy behind the pig-sty. I lit a candle, but yards further, the wind had blown it out and I was in too much of a hurry to relight it. Eventually, I got there, and sat down heavily on the

seat. I put my hands down to be more comfortable and they landed on two roosting hens, one on each side of me. They let off the most terrible cackle. I screamed. The farmyard dogs began barking... I'm certain that the noise would have been heard in the next village. It soon brought my husband at the gallop to see what was going on! Talk about privacy!"

Owen Jones of Llangefni has a stranger tale to tell. He and his family were pestered by a human privy nuisance. Every well-planned privy would face away from the house with a gap of a foot or more for ventilation under or above the door. The opening to theirs faced the low boundary wall between their house and their neighbour's. Their next door neighbour was a retired gent; a widower. His favourite hobby was standing in his garden with his elbows on the wall, his chin cupped in his hands and just staring at their privy door.

If any came to use the privy, he was always there with a greeting, and a little comment about the weather. They all felt that he would be able to hear even the slightest noise they made inside the privy. It was unnerving. But the old man was doing nothing wrong. It was his garden; his boundary wall; and a cat can look at a queen, as they say.

Things came to a head one dark, mid-October evening. Owen Jones explains:-

"My wife decided that before going to bed, she'd need to use the privy. Fair enough.

"I offered to accompany her but she said that she'd be OK if I kept the back-door ajar.

"But I did walk a little way and that was how I knew he was there. I heard him say, 'Evening Missus! Nice one isn't it. Going to rain tomorrow so they say...' I couldn't hear what my wife said to him, but I heard the privy door latch being slammed shut. I moved a little closer knowing that he was there".

"Then there was the most unearthly screech followed by a piercing yell from my wife. I ran towards the loo and saw some wild creature scurrying like a tornado from under the door and jump over the gar-

den wall. I heard a dull thud and the old man next door fell to the ground and rolled down his own garden path.

"It was only after several cups of tea later—laced with brandy—that my wife was able to tell me what had really happened. She had got onto the privy and sat on the seat; she had stretched her arm out in the dark to see if there was paper on the nail. She touched some furry animal, that woke up and had spat at her, before giving a piercing screach, and escaping through the gap under the door. For all she knew, it could have been a fox, a rat, or goodness knows what.

"It was only in the light of the following day that we found that the furry animal had been Simon; the Persian tortoiseshell belonging to Mrs. Williams, Number 6. In his panic to get home—jerked out of his dreams of catching mice and climbing trees—Simon had somersaulted head on into the old pensioner next door and had knocked him clean off his feet. It took the old man months to recover from the shock. But not surprisingly, he never again came and put his elbows on the wall; or passed inane remarks about the weather".

Rats, cats, birds, and hens were all nocturnal visitors to the privy especially on cold winter nights. Hedgehogs, of course, curled in balls on the warm wooden seats. But I have been told by ever so many of my South Wales correspondents that tramps, or gentlemen of the road, would also turn in on cold nights—not to perform—but just to sit and keep dry on a windswept wintry night. Perhaps he was there to muse over the old privy he and his family had had at home, many years ago, and to sense the old smells and the atmosphere of days gone by.

However, it was imperative with privies, even the bravest, even father himself should sing, or whistle, or cough loudly or crunch his feet in the gravel path, to warn clandestine occupants of his coming and give them time to retreat. These were truly adventurous times!

"Gardez l'eau" (see page 25)

Potties at Penrhyn (see page 57)

The 2pm Queue (see page 64)

Smoking Privy (see page 95)

IX

Industrial Privies

❧

Possibly the cosiest, and the snuggest, and the most homely of all the privies I have ever visited is the one, right on my doorstep at Port Penrhyn, Bangor. It is, and fully deserves to be, a listed building. It was built by Lord Penrhyn for the use of the dockers who loaded ships carrying Penrhyn Quarry slates worldwide. This privy was not built haphazardly by any old local builder. This privy was very carefully designed. It is a bespoke, architect designed privy if ever there was one.

The Port Penrhyn 10-seater

It is round and has a very fine slate roof. Inside is the most intricate wrought iron work railings, probably designed and crafted at Penrhyn Quarry's Felin Fawr; the training ground for some of the best sea, and land, engineers in the world. The rails support four massive slate slabs that divide the house into four sections. The first section acts as a vestibule and a one seater privy. The other three sections each house three one-seater privies. It's a glorious 10-seater. Ventilation port holes sit above each hole and the diameter of the round windows are exactly those of the hole seats. This is an aesthetically built loo!

Old Ifan Pugh who used to work as a slate packer in the Port, said to me once, *"You should have heard the debates we used to have in there, Reverend! Some of those debates were far more enthralling, and lively, than most of the ones they had in the House of Commons in London."*

From the beginning of time, Man—and workmen particularly—would urinate and excrete just where and when he felt like it. There would be no question of attempting to cross legs until he came to the nearest public toilet. Nature provided millions of undertaker insects that would nibble, and eat what his body rejected and return it into the earth through their own little bodies. But at some stage in his development, man began to cultivate emotions of shame and modesty and the feeling that it was not for him, a Homo Sapien, to be seen crouching and evacuating himself in public places. So Man decided that he would do his business in a place apart. It was then that all the problems of earth soiling and the emptying of buckets began.

Darwin, in the *'Origin of Species'*, tells us that evolution throughout the world was very uneven. Whilst development on one island almost exploded, it tended to remain static on another. Something similar must have happened in the slate quarries of North Wales!

Pre-War; over 2,000 men worked in the Oakley Quarry in Blaenau Ffestiniog. Approximately half would work in the mills splitting and trim-

Mine entrance Oakley Quarry

ming the slates. The other half worked in the underground caverns, that are now such popular tourist attractions. Terraces of small, open door, privies would be built for these 'shore' men.

The Oakley boasted one of the deepest slate mines in the world, layer upon layer of caverns wending their way deeper and deeper into the ground in a network of tram lines. In that vast, dark underground theatre where 1,000 men worked by candlelight, from seven in the morning till half past four in the afternoon, there was not a single lavatory, or latrine, where a man could stop and do his business. It was pitch dark in those caverns and when the call of nature came, men stopped wherever they were, pulled their trousers down and did it just there … anywhere except on, or between, the tramlines.

It was nature that provided the quarry mine with its own scavengers. Every quarry mine had its thousands of rats and no miner would kill a rat. The men used to walk in couples into the mines; they would link arms and walk the tramlines. Often they would see two small beady eyes coming towards them. The rats also walked the tramlines, and would only give way to their food providers when they were within inches of each other.

I remember a story being told at the time of the appointment of a new under-manager. He was an engineer with no prior experience of slate mines. He was, however, a keen golfer. One day in a lonely part of the mine he took a swipe at a rat coming to meet him. The rat gave out a piercing alarm screach and dozens of other rats rushed to its assistance. The new under-manager had a very lucky escape that day.

I began to wonder if the thousands of miners in the South Wales coal mines were treated any differently from their compatriots in the North. I remember the tales I had heard of the constant danger of leaking gasses, and how the miners would take canaries down the pit to detect these hazards. I asked an old friend of mine, Canon Wynzie Richards. He had worked as a Bevin Boy, during his National Service, at Penycae Colliery, Llandydie, before he entered Lampeter College to become a parson.

I asked him how miners coped with the call of nature two miles or so underground. He told me that there were no latrines below ground … no provision whatsoever. But on the other hand he made the point that there was no problem either. When the call came you just picked up a spade; walked to a quiet spot; performed there; covered it over with coal slack; and away again.

There were rats in plenty down the mines, he told me, and apparently the coal rats had a more varied diet than the slate rats. They all seemed to make their base where the underground ponies were stabled, and enjoyed the same culinary treats as the horses. They did scavenge the miners' latrines, but only when they felt the need for a change of diet. Here, with the ponies, there was warmth and there was plenty of grain and oats to eat.

Canon Richards then recalled a pony called Dai. Dai was a case. His main leisure-time, hobby was rat catching. The men would gather round to see the old rat catcher at work. He would stand perfectly still in his stall, he would close his eyes, and let his head nod every now and again. Then, the men would see a large rat making its way cautiously towards Dai's manger; and still his eyes remained closed; his head remained as if in slumber. Then suddenly, the eyes would blink open, the head would jerk back, and the teeth would snap, and Dai would toss one spine-broken dead rat over his head as far as he could from his stall. Wynzie told me that Dai had probably killed more rats in a month than Neil Jenkins had scored goals in a lifetime.

Then my friend went on to tell me how, one Sunday afternoon, he saw a most amazing thing. The quarry management had decided to move the stables. This was something that was done from time to time. This had been three weeks ago. On this particular Sunday Wynzie saw a battalion of rats marching out of the mine where the old stables had been. They marched regiment by regiment and they were led, so Wynzie tells me, not by the traditional white rat, but by a tawny, ginger rat that deviated neither to the left nor to the right.

I was so interested to hear this tale because when I was a small lad, playing near the Oakley Quarry mine, with two of my playmates, we had witnessed the very same thing. The Oakley quarrymen had been on strike. I can't remember why. Quarrymen don't strike easily, and never for more money, but there had not been a single miner working in the depths of Gloddfa Ganol for the last six weeks. The rats had obviously held a council of war and had decided that they would have to move or starve. They had sent out their scouts to find a new habitation. And when the moving day had come I, and two other boys with me, were there to witness the great trek. To be honest, with the passing of years, I could never be sure whether this was actually something I had seen, or whether it was something that we had made up made up as children. My two mates had been killed in the War, so I couldn't ask them. I have a feeling that our parents and our friends didn't believe our story. I do remember that we had said that the leader was a white rat, and that I had never felt happy about that. I had come to accept that one as a porky. But Wynzie's story brought the memory back; it certainly opened the gates of the sub-conscious. I can now say, that in exactly the same way as Canon Wynzie Richards saw the food-searching evacuation from Llandybie Coal Mine, so my pals and I saw the evacuation of the rats from the Gloddfa Ganol quarry.

Les Sexton of Port Talbot remembers a five-seater in the grounds of Margam Steel works that remained in use until the late 1950s. It was a brick building with a corrugated iron roof. A trench ran under the five seats that had an automatic water valve flushing the lot every five minutes or so. And he remembers the miniskirt doors that allowed the foreman to see and identify the person using the loo, and also his legs to see his trousers were down and that he was not just pretending.

Mrs Winnie Best tells of the industrial loo that was demolished in Milford Haven Docks to make room for the marina, in spite of the efforts of her sister and brother-in-law to have them preserved. These, also, were mounted over a trough of running water. It appear, from what Mrs Best says, that the same old pranks were played in the north and the south of Wales. When it was known that there was someone sitting on one of the seats the jokers outside would light an oil rag and leave it to float towards him, in the little stream, to give him a "hot bottom".

One has the impression that the providing of a private place for the workforce to ease themselves was never regarded by management as a priority.

X

Public Conveniences

The rarest of privies in Wales and the most difficult to find is the public convenience. I have come to the conclusion that this is because not many of them were ever built. One would usually expect to find a good number of the stolid, squarish, Victorian type loo in places like Llandrindod Wells, and our older seaside resorts of Llandudno and Tenby. I have only been able to find two that just about stretch back to the 19th Century. The one set is a pair of rounded brick-work buildings on the Marford Road near Wrexham, and the other is in Cwmdu near Llandeilo.

The Marford twins are listed by CADW and are well looked after. Since my last visit they have had new doors and they had been painted, and the little park around them had been titivated. Unfortunately they sit rather uncomfortably at the edge of their little park. They are on the main road and yet they're not visible from the main road because they are obscured by a rather scraggy shrubbery. This was not their original habitat and I felt it would be good if they could be moved a few feet on to the flatter ground of their park, so that more people would be able to see them and enjoy them, and that they also could be set on a firmer foundation so that they did not give the impression they were about to topple over at any minute.

The pair at Cwmdu have been rescued and renovated by the national Trust. They are a delight. Two little bucket privies set in a meadow just

The Marford Twins (with the authour)

off the road. They have their own little paths leading to them; one for the ladies and the other for the gents, separated by a low stone wall. If they were used today they would probably be a haunt for bisexual rapists waiting in the dark for victims and the council would have to close them.

I have come to the conclusion that our forbears did not use the toilet as often as we do today. The notice found on some privy doors: "Servants may use the privy between the hours of 2pm and 4pm "seems to confirm this.

If we could lay hands on post-mortem reports of people who died 150 years ago, women especially, I feel quite sure we would find that the postmortemees had inordinately large bladders and thick intestines. Young Queen Victoria made such long stage coach journey that one really has to wonder. There was the one trip she made from Wynnstay, near Wrexham, along the A5. They would have stopped in Ceirnoige near Pentrefoelas on the A5 to change horses. The young Queen got out and had tea in the farm house. There is a plaque on the wall that reports this incident. She would then have travelled, changing horses every seven miles, to Beaumaris. In her older days the Queen lived dangerously. She very nearly waited too long, on the High Street in Bala, Merionethshire before telling her ladies in waiting, that she needed the toilet. Her ladies scurried around and found a suitable place inside the Royal Hotel. I think it is quite true that the queen did use the toilet at the White Lion. This is how it became known by the rather twisted name of "The White Lion Royal Hotel". In most other hotel names where Royal precedes the name, The Royal Sportsman, The Royal Waterloo, I have been told that the title of "Royal "is given by monarch's warrant to all who sell goods, or service, by appointment to the monarch. When the Queen came to Bala the call was so urgent there was no time to make an appointment; it was an emergency. This, I am told, is why the White Lion in the Main Street in Bala has to make do with its rather unusual, semi official title of White Lion Royal Hotel. Or has someone been pulling my leg?

The sedate Ladies and Gentlemen at Cwm Du

The White Lion Royal Hotel, Bala

But Royal White Lion or not the Queen did visit various taverns to make herself comfortable. A hundred years later her subjects, when they visit foreign countries are doing exactly the same thing. Public Conveniences are so few and far between in Turkey and in Greece and in other European countries that if there was not another, alternative way of relieving oneself, one would simply have to stay at home. But like the old Queen, the seasoned traveller will pop into one of the countless tavernas in these countries, saunter up to the bar and order a drink, ask the way to the toilet, and hey presto.

This is exactly what seasoned travellers on our roads, would have done, in the days of the Stage Coaches. They would have gone into the tavern both for refreshment and for easement. There was no choice because many of the longer journeys required overnight stays. Then, almost at the same time that Stage Coach travel gave place to the railways,

Wales was rocked by its many religious revivals and its temperance campaigns. Taverns became the dwelling place of the devil and only scarlet women were known to enter. The tavern doors were suddenly closed to all the women and, except for the back door, to many respectable church and chapel male members. When the tavern doors were closed to teetotallers their toilet doors were also shut to the incontinent. The religious revival effect still remains; there is a great deal of difference even today, between the going "Down to my local" of the Englishman, and then "Mynd i' r dafarn" of the Welshman. I began to wonder if this had any connection with something a fellow clergyman said to me. He had moved to a parish in Wales after serving many years in England. He said:- "I'll tell you the greatest difference I find between the Welsh and the English members of my congregation. When I chat to them at the end of the service, English members will invariably say that they are off to see friends or to have coffee with friends. Welsh members of my congregation will just as invariably say that they are off to call on his mother, or her sister's family."

Are we more family minded in Wales or is this a throw back to the lack of public convenience days? Those days when you knew that if you moved anywhere away from your own home you would be wise to move to family, where you and your own would be able to use their privy provided you used it sparingly.

XI

Restorations and Renovations

❧

This is a joy chapter in the history of privies. We can pause here and sing to the Cliff Richards' tune "Congratulations and Celebrations". Many of our old privies are being carefully repaired and renovated. "Restorations and Renovations". There was a time just after the war when auctioneers would accept a £1 for a grandfather's clock, and a fiver would buy a good solid oak Welsh Dresser. Gradually the antiques men stepped in and prices spiralled. But strangely they all spiralled except the poor old Welsh Dresser. The Welsh Dresser remained the orphan Annie of the antiques trade for many years. But when it did come into its own it came with a vengeance. Even for the sickest looking and the most decrepit of dressers today the bidding never starts under £2,000. Similarly I have a feeling that, at long last, the attitude towards old privies is also on the turn. The younger people are just beginning to say that it's 'cool' and even 'wicked' to possess one's own olden days privy at the bottom of the garden. I have been invited to visit many renovated privies, and privies in the process of being given a new life.

The first I was invited to inspect was at Pentir Old Vicarage, Carrog, on the banks of the River Dee. The old privy had been incorporated into a covered barbeque/picnic area. The only pity was that the old dove cote in the original building, had to be confiscated. But the back quarters has a lovely little corner loo for the servants that has been well preserved with a new slate roof.

Before and after—Old Vicarage Pentir

I also found Gerald Barber, a retired surveyor, hard at it renovating his three-seater at Tal y Cafn Isaf, Llanfihangel Glyn Myfyr.

The privy at Gilfach Goch farm, Llanbedr, near Barmouth was not in need of renovation. It had been built as an earth privy, two hundred years ago, and looked strong enough to withstand another two hundred.

We are also very greatly indebted to the National Trust, for

Gilfach Goch, Llanbedr, Barmouth

the love they show for all things old and beautiful. Their enterprise at Llanerchaeron, near Lampeter, Ceredigion, is well worth a visit. This is a place where they are giving the kiss of life to a village manor and its surrounding homes, built by John Nash, 1794-96. Nicky Evans, the site archaeologist, tells me that work is now in progress to renovate privy N 20019. The superstructure is very damaged but not beyond repair to these people who never give up. The long drop from it to the stream below, a drop of about 2 meters, is still intact. The National Trust has also resuscitated for us the little hamlet of Cwm Du, near Llandeilo with its quaint public convenience.

But Mrs A.G. Williams of Cwmgwrach, Neath, told me the sad story of the privy that was allowed to die. This old closet was described, in the local newspapers ten years ago as:- *"The Loneliest Loo in Wales"*; and it was allowed to die.

In May 1989 the people of Resolven read an article in the 'Herald of

The big drop at Llanerchafron

Herald of Wales, Thursday, May 18, 1989 3

Cadw to list it?

THE loneliest loo in Wales may soon become a protected building.

Officers from Cadw will be paying a visit to the circular stone privy, nearly a thousand feet up a mountainside at Rheola, to see if it is worth listing as an architectural curiosity.

Wales' that brought great joy. It said; *"Officers from CADW will be paying a visit to the circular stone privy nearly a thousand feet up the mountainside at Rheola to see if it is worth having it listed as an architectural curiosity"*. Obviously the officers never arrived because if they had, and they had seen this gorgeous little privy, with its stone built conical roof, as it was then, it would have been renovated and listed and would be still alive today. Dr Eurwyn William of the Welsh Folk Museum is also reported as having said of it: *"There is nothing else quite like it. To my knowledge it is quite unique. There are two or three round stone lavatories in the old estate village of Marford in Flintshire. But they are architect designed and not such fine examples."* What a pity his colleagues didn't send a lorry, there and then, to cart this unique little privy away to St Fagans for rebuilding because ten years ago it didn't seem to belong to anyone. The farm it had served for over a hundred years had been pulled down, and it was left an orphan. The two architect-designed circular lavatories at Marford were listed and are still in a good state of preservation. But today little remains of this lovely circular old loo with its stone dome-shaped stone roof.

But I have found a similar one, not quite as old, not quite as cleverly built, but still nostalgic to look at. This one is in the grounds of a lovely old mansion house Prysgaeddfed in Bodedern, Anglesey. I had a feeling that this one looks worse than it really is. The little building is infested with ivy. I'm sure that if the ivy was carefully removed the whole building would perk up no end. Mark, my son, discovered the missing panel from its inside, in the woods, probably blown out during the recent gales. We put it back where it belonged.

Prysgaeddfed Hall, Bodedern "worth preserving "

I have often addressed meetings of Historical Societies that have attendances of over a hundred at every monthly meeting. Many members think nothing of travelling long distances to listen to lectures about the happenings of the past. I have often thought what a wonderful idea it would be if just ten percent of these members formed themselves into a sort of Guild of St James. I say St James because he was the evangelist that exhorted all to "Be ye doers of the word and not hearers only". How wonderful if we had in every area a branch of the "Guild of St James—Privy Restorers". Just three people could restore many of them in a matter of hours especially if one had a smattering of gardening skills to cut off the ivy and another had D.I.Y. skills with a trowel and a bit of mortar.

Benar Penmachno "Pedigree"

Of course many of our old privies, in Wales, have been repaired and registered as listed buildings by CADW. There is that lovely one in Benar Penmachno, Conwy. The listed privies are of course the pedigree ones. Like Crufts champions they have their pedigree papers. I asked to see the papers of the Benar Privy and it read;-

"Lavatory drops steeply down to a stream at the house, probably mid C19. Local flat rubble: thick slate roof. Centrally placed double wooden doors. Gable end to NW and SE; that to SE has a small window. Building built into slope of ground in rear. Stream flows through square headed openings in the lower part of gable walls. Interior has two seater latrine with wooden seats overhanging stream which carried away waste".

All the listed buildings, be they castles, churches, mansions, merchant houses, or privies carry these papers. To destroy, or deface, or in any way to disfigure, a listed building is a criminal offence. The beautiful Dove Loft-Privy at Abercamlais is a listed building, as are also the wonderful examples of circular privies at Porth Penrhyn and at Marford Hill on the Wrexham Road.

But it is not just the privies of the nobler homes that have been listed. Mrs Mair Reed who was brought up in Ty Isaf where her mother was born in 1908, writes to tell me that her father in 1996 sold the farm when he was 93 years of age. She also tells me that the old privy has since been listed and goes on to say:- "How nice it is for our family to know that the new owners are doing everything to preserve Ty Isaf."

It would be wonderful if our remaining loos could be given the same privilege and have their own papers to prove it. But this must remain a pipe dream. CADW has so many old buildings to care for and so few carers to do the caring. I would, however, think that where a community has got together to repair, and rebuild, a particular old building, they would have the right to ask CADW to come and inspect their work, and to consider listing it, so that it would not so easily fall prey to future vandals.

The repaired seat

I think Mr Edward James of Pembrey, Burry Port, would be very much within his rights if he did this. They have in their garden a rather staid and prissy suburban privy that was built the same time as the house over 200 years ago; but it looks much younger than its years. Mr James's renovating has been methodically precise. The experts from CADW could not have done better. Part of the original seat had perished, and so a local carpenter was called in to splice a new end to the old. The tiled floor was raised cleaned and replaced. The new window frame is exactly like the old. The privy stands now as proudly and as elegantly as it did two hundred years ago. Mr James has, obviously, a good knowledge of privies.

He told me that he was now on the look out for a couple of real privy buckets to place under the holed seat. Many of the privy books that I have read show pictures of privy buckets. But most of the pictures shown are of any old buckets or scuttles. I have only seen one book that shows the picture of the real privy bucket, made specially for the job.

It has a short handle (anti-splash device) and a long body (to allow for a seven day loading). When this type of privy bucket will have been found, and installed, Mr James will have restored his privy into its pristine condition. He will have made it look exactly as it did look when it was first built. I think this one would deserve its pedigree papers as a perfect example of a suburban bucket privy. A listing would guarantee that no vandal successor to the property could ever bulldoze Mr James' work to the ground, to find space for a second garage, or a garden tool house.

A young look for this aged Penbrey privy

NOTE BENE

There is still more cause for celebration. Recently Estate Agents, always on the look out for any features that will put up the price of the property they are selling, have found that to have a 250 year old privy in good condition in the garden, enhances the sale. Often recently, a bottom of the garden loo is described in the house bumph as if it was pedigree listed—with just a hint, at the end, that it may need a little attention.

A real Privy Bucket

XII

The Smoking Privy

It was Mrs. Muriel Parry, from Lleyn, who told me this story. Muriel and I have known each other for many, many years. When she heard I was writing a book about privies, she thought it only right I should have a good privy mystery to include in it.

Muriel told me that before the First World War, her uncle Tom, her mother's brother, had married a most peculiar woman. She was reputed to have come from South Wales. She certainly spoke as they do in the South, but apart from that no one knew a thing about her or how Uncle Tom had come to lay eyes on her. Tom was the first volunteer from the village to answer Kitchener's Call. Many said, "with good reason"— Matilda's constant nagging. He came home five years later a sick and broken man. When he died as a result of his war wounds six years later, he and Matilda had four children.

Matilda was sadistic in the way she treated her children; she threatened them, she beat them, and she meted out the most horrible of punishments for the most minor misdemeanours. And she was especially hard on Maldwyn. Maldwyn was the youngest and he was a little slow. He was terrified of his mother and had developed such a stutter that no one, except his grandfather, could understand a word he said. Maldwyn loved his grandfather who lived near them, and when he was with him he could converse without the slightest impediment.

The children grew up and left home to go as domestics and farm labourers with the same alacrity that their father had joined the army. Matilda bought the village shop and used Maldwyn to haul the groceries on and off the shelves and to dig the garden so that they had garden produce to sell. Even when Maldwyn was a young man, the constant nagging went on, but at least the beatings had stopped. It was around Maldwyn's 30th birthday that it happened. Matilda had been acting strangely, arranging and re-arranging the shelves long after closing time. One day, a customer came in and complained that he had bought a packet of ten Woodbines the previous day and when he had taken it home and opened it, it had one cigarette missing.

There were similar complaints from customers the next day and what's more, pipe-smokers began complaining that their packets of shag had been tampered with. Matilda blamed Maldwyn. She even took a stick and beat her poor, terrified son as he pleaded his innocence with her.

That night, Maldwyn crossed the road and visited his grandfather. "Honest, Grandpa", he said, "I have never smoked in my life. It's her that's pinching the cigarettes and the 'bacco'. I know she smokes cigarettes and she's also got a clay pipe."

"How do you know?" asked Grandpa.

"Well, I've seen the clay pipe in her apron pocket," said Maldwyn, "and when she goes to the privy after tea, you can see the smoke coming out from under the door and through the little window".

"Does she go in the privy the same time every day, Maldwyn?" enquired Grandpa.

"Yes; five o'clock every night. Regular!"

"Right," said Grandpa, "this is what we must do to catch her red-handed; and you, Maldwyn, will have to do most of this yourself."

"Fill a bucket with cold water and hide it behind the privy. When you see your mother heading for the privy, go round the back to where the bucket is. As soon as you see the smoke, but not before mind, grab your bucket, kick the privy door open, and throw the water over whoever is sitting on the seat. Do you understand me Maldwyn?"

"Throw the water over whoever is sitting on the seat!" he repeated.

"But Grandpa, she'll kill me...!" whined Maldwyn.

"No, lad," said the co-conspirator, "I will be there. I will have taken my place behind the old apple tree. But you see, Maldwyn, she must be caught red-handed before anyone will believe you. I shall be your witness."

"But..." began a terrified Maldwyn.

"But nothing!" said his grandfather. "If she says anything you will just have to say,' I threw the water because I thought the privy was on fire'."

The plan worked. Matilda went to the loo at the usual time. Maldwyn took his place by the bucket of water. From where he stood he could just see the peak of his Gramp's cap behind the apple tree. There was a wait of a few minutes then billows of smoke came from under the privy door and through the tiny little window. Maldwyn sprang into action, kicked the door open and heaved the bucketful of water in the direction of the privy seat. In seconds Grandpa, his witness, was standing there by his side. There was no sound from Matilda. She just sat there soaking wet, with her thin white hair falling in wet wisps down her awe struck face. The limp woodbine cigarette was still in place between her lips, and the clay pipe and the box of baccy was on the seat beside her.

Matilda apparently never really recovered from her near drowning experience.

Muriel also told me that Maldwyn, aged 82, retired recently as the rather prosperous owner /manager of the village store

XIII

And I am the Epilogue - Privus Aelwynis

The Epilogue in every book is that final chapter that is meant to calm the nerves of those aroused by its stirring ideas and its inspiring innovations. This epilogue is different; it compounds the mystery.

It all began soon after I had published, "The Privies of North Wales". A good friend of many years said to me, "Had I known you were writing a book about privies, I would have asked you to come over and see my little beauty." So when I came to write my second privy book I invited myself to see it. And there he was sitting in his retirement, in the farmhouse conservatory, holding within his bosom an aspidistra in pot. I had never before seen anything like it.

It was made of cast iron and showed evidence of generations of blackleading. It stood on four flat feet which bore the holes made for the bolts and nuts that, in its working days, were to hold it firmly to the floor. It had the appearance of a witches' cauldron. Inside the cauldron thing there was a carefully crafted, hinged, copper basin attached to a handle. When the handle was lifted the copper basin tipped its contents into a wide mouthed pipe at the base of the cauldron. The wide mouthed pipe carried its contents under the floor boards, through a hole in the outside wall, and into a bucket standing in the yard below. Presumably the contents would then be emptied by the gardener and thrown over the potato patch. I should have added that this was a closet that would only have operated from a bedroom or a second floor level. It was basically simple. You went upstairs to the toilet just as you do today; you lower the seat on to the cast iron pan; you do your business into the copper basin; you lift the lever which tips the contents of the copper pan into the wide mouthed pipe. You then manually pour a little water, from a jug attachment, to cleanse the copper pan, and more water to dispatch the contents to the bucket below. It is really a wonderful invention. There would be no more cold nightly walk abouts to the top of the garden. No smells; and as an added bonus the bucket contents could be recycled into valuable garden manure.

I had never before seen or heard of a cast iron lavatory pan. Nor had I imagined such an ingenious contrivance as the one my friend called his "Long Drop Closet". Provided one did not live in a bungalow this particular toilet had everything. I knew I had to find the innovator of this simple but efficient device.

The clue, I thought, could be in the handle. Inscribed on the porcelain handle were the words JOHN JONES, PLUMBER, CARNARVON. This could mean a lot or nothing at all. I remember my father used to have a bicycle with the name of the Blaenau Ffestiniog retailer and his address embellished on the bar. No bike was ever devised or built in Blaenau. The man whose name adorned the bicycle bar was the maker's agent in Blaenau. I suspected that John Jones, Plumber, Carnarvon was also an agent for this unique closet.

I consulted the experts. I sent photographs to CADW, Ancient Monuments, The Victoria and Albert and St Fagans. CADW had never heard of it or of anything resembling it. Ancient Monuments circulated copies

Privus Aelwynis, showing tipping handle

The Privus Aelwynis

of the photograph amongst its staff but no ideas were forthcoming. The Victoria and Albert were busy Spring Cleaning and unable to answer any queries for weeks to come. St Fagan however had heard of cast iron closets. They had come across one at Waterton Hall near Bridgend. They told me that it had probably been installed in the Hall when Madam Patti rented it for two years whilst her home, "Craig y Nos", was being built.

But the Madam Patti loo had a Cummings Valve and was also fed from a ceiling water tank. The only thing it had in common with my little loo (I am already beginning to think of it as my little loo) was the fact they both had a cast iron pan instead of a ceramic pan. I called at the Iron Gorge Museum in Telford. The registrar was able to tell me of a great variety of cast iron closet pans. But like our good friends at St Fagans he too had to admit that all the ones he knew about had the Cummings Valve and were water fed from a ceiling tank.

At this point I appealed through the newspapers of Wales for information. In my letter I unashamedly admitted that if no one could supply information, and give the name of the innovator of this great contraption, I would be claiming patent rights for it and would name it *Privus Aelwynis*. This was two months before the book manuscript was handed in to the publisher. There hasn't been a squeak. It has been suggested that as my version has no Cummings valve attachment it could be pre Cummings (1775). I doubt this very much because its cast iron cauldron body is far too like the ones produced one hundred years later.

It could be that some cunning Welshman found a Cummings type pan in a dump, stripped it of its valve and adapted it for use from an upper story bedroom, on the long drop principle. But no. My *Privus Aelwynis* shows no evidence that it has ever at any time been connected to a ceiling water tank. There seems to be no one in this wide world able to gainsay me if I venture to suggest that, perhaps, the message on the rather posh porcelain handle is the correct one—that this particular privy, for second floor use, was produced, sold, and installed by John Jones, Plumber, of Caernarfon. He could have had the pans cast for him at Felin Fawr Foundry in the Penrhyn Quarries or the equally famous foundry at Porthmadog.

So mysteries still abound. My old friend Chloris Morgan has already written to me suggesting that I should think of adding a third volume to the privy series. This one would be entitled "The Privies of the World". I have my suspicion that Chloris Morgan would willingly pay the price of a third volume simply in order to have the answer to a question that has intrigued her for years:- "Do igloos have indoor toilets? If not how is it possible for Eskimos to bare their nether parts outdoors in temperatures of 50 degrees below without suffering grievous bodily harm?" It is something well worth thinking about.

Retired 100 years ago and still handsome, in an ugly sort of way